Scrapbooks on the Go

Collect & Create While You Travel

C&T PUBLISHING

Jan Bode Smiley

Text © 2006 Jan Bode Smiley

Artwork © 2006 C&T Publishing, Inc.

Publisher: Amy Marson

Editorial Director: Gailen Runge

Acquisitions Editor: Jan Grigsby

Editor: Stacy Chamness

Copyeditor/Proofreader: Wordfirm Inc.

Cover Designer/Design Director/Book Designer: Kristen Yenche

Production Assistant: Kirstie L. Pettersen

Photography: C&T Publishing, Inc., unless otherwise noted

Stock Photography: PhotoSpin

Published by C&T Publishing, Inc., P.O. Box 1456, Lafayette, CA 94549

Attention Teachers: C&T Publishing, Inc., encourages you to use this book as a text for teaching. Contact us at 800-284-1114 or www.ctpub.com for more information about the C&T Teachers Program.

We take great care to ensure that the information included in our books is accurate and presented in good faith, but no warranty is provided nor results guaranteed. Having no control over the choices of materials or procedures used, neither the author nor C&T Publishing, Inc., shall have any liability to any person or entity with respect to any loss or damage caused directly or indirectly by the information contained in this book. For your convenience, we post an up-to-date listing of corrections on our website (www.ctpub.com). If a correction is not already noted, please contact our customer service department at ctinfo@ctpub.com or at P.O. Box 1456, Lafayette, CA, 94549.

Trademark (™) and registered trademark (®) names are used throughout this book. Rather than use the symbols with every occurrence of a trademark or registered trademark name, we are using the names only in the editorial fashion and to the benefit of the owner, with no intention of infringement.

Library of Congress Cataloging-in-Publication Data

Smiley, Jan Bode

  Scrapbooks on the go : collect & create while you travel / Jan Smiley.

    p. cm.

  ISBN-13: 978-1-57120-365-6 (paper trade)

  ISBN-10: 1-57120-365-6 (paper trade)

  1. Photograph albums. 2. Scrapbooks. 3. Travel photography. 4. Travel paraphernalia. I. Title.

  TR501.S59 2006

  745.593—dc22

2005035311

Printed in Singapore

10 9 8 7 6 5 4 3 2 1

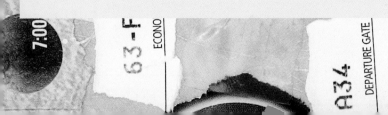

Acknowledgments

Thanks to the C&T team for their incredible support. It's been a great relationship, and I look forward to continuing to work with such talented people. Stacy, you've been awesome to work with!

Dedication

To Tom—thanks for the travel opportunities. I look forward to documenting more time together.

To Emma and Keith—the best kids a mom could hope for!

To book artists, journal lovers, and scrapbook artists, both novice and experienced: I hope that this book will expand your ideas on ways to document your journey and that you will enjoy the process and the unexpected discoveries along the way as much as I do!

table of contents

Do these overflowing boxes of photographs look familiar?

iNtroductioN

Create a Travel Scrapbook Before Getting Home

Many of us face a similar challenge: lots of photographs, lots of memories, lots of big ideas, but a limited amount of time to execute our ideas. Instead of coming home from your next vacation, bridal shower, birthday party, trip to the beach, or family reunion with a pile of photos and ephemera to honor the event, follow the examples shared in this book to create your scrapbook the same day as the event—while the energy and excitement are still with you.

How many times have you returned from a wonderful vacation or family reunion full of enthusiasm to get your scrapbook together to commemorate the experience? Then, a week or more later, you finally get your photos developed or printed.

By that time, you are back in your normal routine: laundry, cooking, work, family schedules to maintain … the list continues, right? Life moves so fast that we are often on to the next thing before we've documented the last wonderful event that happened.

Instead of allowing those piles of photographs to continue multiplying in front of your eyes—making you feel incredibly guilty for not having done anything with them yet—create a Scrapbook on the Go! You'll be amazed how easy it is to incorporate the spontaneity of each day into your project.

No more guilt—let's scrapbook on the go!

Scrapbooks on the go kit

You're thinking that this Scrapbook on the Go idea just might work for you, right? What next? How do you get started? What do you need to have? Let's start with three essential items and then add to your Scrapbook on the Go kit from there, based in part on your interests and budget.

The Essentials

Camera

Whether it be digital, 35mm, disposable, or even Polaroid, any type of camera will do for your Scrapbook on the Go.

Any camera will work for your Scrapbook on the Go.

Plan to process your photos along the way. Here are some of your options:

- Depending on your scrapbooking budget, you might buy a portable photo printer with the appropriate paper and ink cartridges. See Sources on page 63 for more information on this option.

- Take advantage of the many one-hour photo-processing labs you'll come across in your travels.

- Print your digital images at one of the machines popping up in malls, grocery stores, drugstores, and photo-processing kiosks.

- Use a Polaroid camera so that your photos will develop immediately after you take them and you won't need any additional equipment.

- Bring prepared blank board books (page 23) and simply work with your ephemera on the trip. You can place your photos once you return home!

A Type of Base

- A purchased scrapbook or a blank board book. Be sure to choose a size that is both practical to transport and pleasing to work in. For a single event, tiny sizes can be fun to use.

- A purchased papier-mâché box from the craft store. Again, remember to select a size that will be practical for your project. Cute as it might be, a tiny box probably won't be big enough to hold your photos.

- A recycled cigar box or a favorite decorative tin.

- Maybe some envelopes bound together or recycled file folders and decorative papers. Throughout this book, you'll see many more options for portable scrapbooks, including paper and metal boxes, envelopes, and even brown paper lunch bags.

A variety of base options for your Scrapbook on the Go

We'll explore many of these options in depth later on. Using a variety of bases for your Scrapbooks on the Go will keep you excited about the process, so continue to look for shapes, sizes, and unique items that might work for future Scrapbooks on the Go.

A Plan

- Having a plan makes everything fall into place. If you know what direction you want to take with your book, you can easily get across the feeling you want to invoke.

Easy Additions

Now that you have your essential elements, you can add to your Scrapbook on the Go kit based on the event or trip you are planning, your budget, and your personal taste. Here are some general items to consider adding to your kit, many of which you probably already have on hand:

Background paper—See Paper Pizzazz (pages 18–22), for a discussion about background papers.

A variety of scrapbook papers

Note

Don't feel that you can't be successful with your Scrapbook on the Go without scrapbook paper. As wonderful and tempting as scrapbook paper is, you can have fun and be creative with other types of paper as well. Several examples in this book incorporate found papers and other paper sources.

Adhesives for photos and ephemera—A glue stick, masking tape, double-stick tape, or colored tape to adhere your items to your scrapbook. Remember to choose an archival, acid-free product if that characteristic is important to you. If you like to pick up trinkets like rusty metal, shells, and small rocks, you'll want to include an adhesive that can handle them. If you don't already have a favorite, try The Ultimate! adhesive from Crafter's Pick. (See Sources on page 63.)

Tip — Small pieces of vintage paper, lined notebook or ledger paper, and left-over pieces of scrapbook paper you like are great for journaling and for adding interest and variety to your pages. You can use them for things like matting your photos, stamping titles, and mounting extra collage pieces.

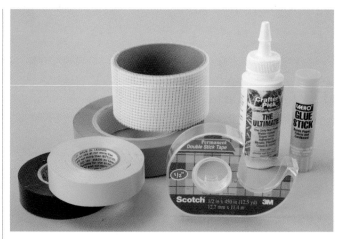

A variety of adhesives and tape

Scissors—If you want straight edges. Otherwise, tearing paper for your pages results in an interesting soft edge that might enhance your layout. Decorative-edge scissors are fun and more forgiving of cuts that are less than perfectly straight. You'll see examples of these techniques throughout the projects in this book.

Pens for journaling—Test each pen to be sure it will write on your papers. See Sources on page 63 for some of my personal favorites. Regular pencils write on a wide variety of surfaces, too.

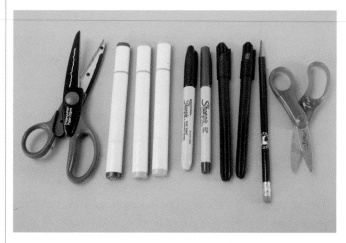

Include scissors and pens in your Scrapbook on the Go kit.

Ephemera—You will collect plenty of ephemera on your journey. To get started or to ensure variety, put a vintage label maker, some labels, label holders, miniature file folders, tiny envelopes, fasteners, and so on in a small, resealable plastic bag and add it to your kit.

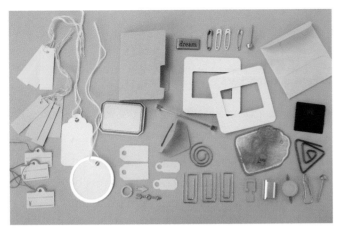

A variety of easy-to-add trinkets for your Scrapbook on the Go kit

- Rub-on letters, which are easy to use and come in a variety of fonts, sizes, and colors
- Rub-on words, which are available in themed sets
- Small stamp pads for direct-to-paper techniques
- Markers, chalk, color pencils, and paints for added color
- Embellishments that fit your theme (e.g., metal letters to spell out a place or person's name, or stickers with an appropriate theme)
- Slide mounts to frame a favorite photo
- Envelopes in which you can tuck journaling, extra photos, and ephemera
- A small stapler and some staples (You can even buy colored staples for those little staplers now.)

> **Tip** If archival issues are important to you, consider adding a bottle of Archival Mist spray (see Sources on page 63) to your traveling Scrapbook on the Go kit.

> **Tip** I almost always add an envelope or pocket somewhere in my scrapbooks. Envelopes and pockets provide the perfect place to put those extra photos and collected items that aren't quite special enough to arrange on a page but that you just can't part with (leftover brochures, maps, postcards, and other memories).

The Kitchen Sink?

Don't try to take everything but the kitchen sink with you on the road. Be reasonable when packing your kit, especially if you are flying or traveling with other people. Nothing will turn off your family and friends to your Scrapbook on the Go project faster than asking them to carry your 50-pound suitcase of scrapbook supplies. Trust me on this.

Just remember that you can always add more embellishments when you get home.

The Extras: Optional Items to Spice Up Your Kit

Optional extras are endless, but here are some to consider. What you include might depend on factors such as available space and the length of the trip or event:

- A rubber stamp alphabet and a stamp pad for creating titles on your pages

> **Tip** If you worry about ruining your scrapbook page by making a mistake while stamping text, simply stamp onto a separate piece of paper, and then glue that piece onto your spread after the ink is dry.

Remember to keep it simple as you get started on your Scrapbook on the Go kit. Often I find I am most creative when forced to make do with what I have available. Sometimes too many choices slow me down as I try to figure out which one is best. Make the process easier by limiting what you pack ahead of time and forcing yourself to be creative within these limits. Try it!

Note

When traveling recently, I decided I wanted to paint some dots on my canvas page. Aha! A pencil eraser is a great dot maker. I used it to make several dots on my pages. Then I thought I'd like some bigger dots. What did I have available? Hmmm … a wine bottle cork? Nope, too big and solid for this page. Oh! The bottom of a fingernail polish bottle would make perfect dots! Cool! I would never have thought of using that if I'd been at home in my studio. It took the limited resources available in my hotel room to make me really look around and realize that I had exactly what I needed right in the room with me.

art packing list

I got tired of reinventing the wheel every time I packed my art supplies for a trip, so I finally created an art packing list. (It's especially helpful when I actually remember to look at it before I leave home!)

Using this basic art packing list as a starting point, make one for yourself that fits the way you like to work and your favorite supplies. The list includes a few lines at the end for you to customize based on your personal preferences. After a trip or two, you'll have your personal list refined and ready for any spur-of-the-moment event.

❏ **Camera** It can be digital, 35mm, or Polaroid—any working camera with the appropriate film or memory card and batteries will do.

❏ **A book to work in** Sometimes I do something to the book before the trip, and other times I take it along just as I bought it. Still other times I buy something to work in early in the trip and start my Scrapbook on the Go feeding off the energy of a new purchase.

❏ **One or more small inkpads and a rubber stamp alphabet or rub-on letters** Small inkpads can also be used to highlight and color the edges of your pages and your collage ephemera or to completely change the color of a found paper that you want to include on your page.

❏ **Envelopes, tags, pockets, and bags** If you are a collector, as I am, and like to pick up treasures such as pebbles, shells, feathers, and rusty metal, add a few small, resealable plastic bags to your Scrapbook on the Go kit. You'll be happy not to have all that sand or rust fall into the bottom of your purse or pocket. Need I say more?

❏ **Small scissors** I usually don't have any problems at airport security checkpoints with blunt-tip scissors in my carry-on luggage—think primary school safety scissors. If you are checking luggage, you can pack regular scissors. Alternately, another handy-dandy tool is a 6″ metal-edge ruler. You can tear straight edges against the side of the ruler and not worry about anyone confiscating your tools!

❏ **Pens and markers**

• Pens for journaling and keeping track of your adventures. I like Nexus pens (see Sources on page 63).

• I love Copic markers (see Sources on page 63) for versatility and color selection. I carry about three colors on a trip. Which colors I take varies from trip to trip.

• Sharpie markers are very versatile for writing on different surfaces. The ones that have an extra-fine tip at one end and a regular tip on the other are great.

• Pencils. Yes, regular pencils, like those you used in grade school, are very versatile and great for adding some personal marks to your Scrapbook on the Go pages. Using mechanical pencils means you don't have to carry a pencil sharpener along. I like thicker lead because I'm less likely to break it and it makes a nice bold line.

❏ **Adhesives** A glue stick and a strong all-around adhesive are invaluable. Pick an archival, acid-free product for results that won't discolor with age. My favorite is The Ultimate! (see Sources on page 63). Double-sided tape is very handy, too.

❏ **Tape** I am tape obsessed. I've been this way for years. My family has given up on trying to cure me. Think colored masking tape, colored electrical tape, colored duct tape, colored book-making tape, colored construction tape, and drywall tape. Scrapbook companies are now making decorative tapes for us, so I guess I'm not the only one who is tape obsessed! Include clear packing tape if you want to do any packing-tape transfers, as shown on page 32.

❏ **Portable printer** A portable printer is optional.

❏ **Small pieces of paper for journaling and then placing in your book** Leftover bits of scrapbook paper, vintage notebook paper, colored memo paper—anything you're comfortable writing on is perfect.

❏ **A small watercolor set, water-soluble oil pastels, or a small set of colored pencils** Depending on your interests, you might consider adding some or all of these. Look in teacher supply stores, dollar stores, and art supply stores for miniature sets, which are very portable, as well as affordable.

❏ **An open mind** Be open to changing your plan once you leave home. What seemed like the perfect idea when you packed might be replaced by something new, wonderful, and inspired by the event or trip. Acknowledge the new ideas, and incorporate them into your book for a truly special, spontaneous Scrapbook on the Go!

❏ **Other items I need for this trip/event:**

❏ _____

❏ _____

❏ _____

❏ _____

Tip I use a clear plastic zipper pouch to carry my supplies. Any resealable bag is good: things don't slip out, and you can easily find what you're looking for without emptying the entire bag. If you're flying, the see-through pouch makes it easier for airport security to see what you're carrying.

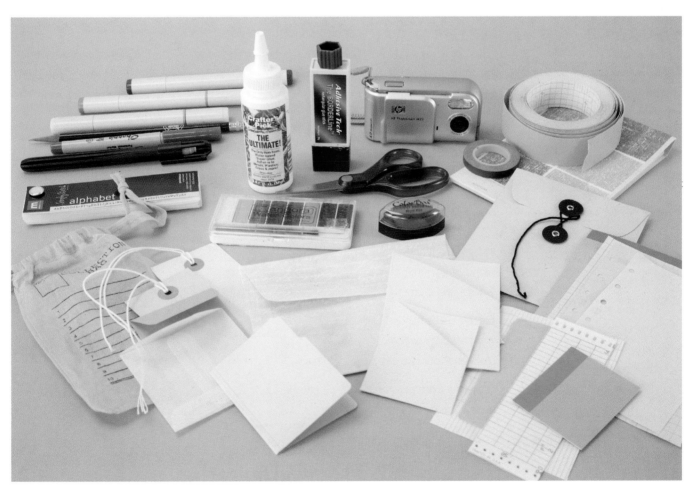

Art supplies ready for almost anything

collecting along the way

Whether you are actually creating your Scrapbook on the Go while you're still on the go or you are collecting along the way to create when you get home, here are some ideas for what to collect and how to keep it organized.

Collecting free stuff for a Scrapbook on the Go

I'm always on the lookout for free stuff when I travel. Not only does it save me money, but these "found" items add a lot of interest to my Scrapbooks on the Go. You'll see examples throughout the finished scrapbooks in this book. Refer back to this list just before a trip so you'll remember what to start collecting.

Free Stuff to Collect

- Maps

  They make great backgrounds for your page.

  They're great reminders of where you were when you took those photographs.

  You can use them as references for the spelling and names of places along the way.

  It's fun to highlight your travel route and include it in your scrapbook.

- In-flight magazines—a wonderful source of maps, words, and images

- Freebie items handed out in places like shopping malls and tourist areas

- Packaging from purchases, such as candy wrappers or souvenirs

- Receipts

- Interesting logos from bags

- Tissue paper from purchases, which can be used to make an interesting textured background or to cover a tag in your Scrapbook on the Go

- Business cards from restaurants, hotels, and shops

- Coasters and napkins

- Coffee cup cozies

- Train, subway, and ferry maps and schedules

- Tickets stubs from subway, ferry, train, and airline trips

- Luggage tags

- Found objects

  Shells

  Rocks

  Beach glass

  Feathers

  Metal objects

  Butterfly and moth wings

  Flower petals

  Leaves

  Ephemera

- Brochures

  They're great folded and included in your book.

  They serve as good references for later, when you want to remember details about a place.

  They're a wonderful source for words and images to cut out.

  They are a great source of images for hard-to-photograph areas.

  They can show a time of day when you didn't get a photograph.

- Bottle caps, labels, or wine bottle corks

- Passport stamps, such as those found in national park visitor centers

days Tip Don't stop with just a stamp in your National Parks Passport; be sure to stamp a few extra images so you can include one in your Scrapbook on the Go. Better yet, carry your scrapbook with you, and stamp directly on your page.

Refer to Drying Plant Material in Your Microwave (page 44) to learn how to handle your flowers and leaves.

Use a craft knife to cut wine bottle corks in half lengthwise before gluing them to your page to reduce the bulk inside your book.

Fun Stuff to Buy When Traveling

We all know that not everything worth having is free. Some inexpensive items are a lot of fun to search for (and buy) when you are traveling. You save money by purchasing inexpensive souvenirs instead of big-ticket items. You have something new and unique to use right away in your Scrapbook on the Go, and best of all, you don't need to find a place to put it once you get home. It's already been incorporated into your book. No unpacking souvenirs, and no new clutter to deal with once you get home!

Inexpensive items for your Scrapbook on the Go

Soak the label off a bottle by filling the bottle with hot water and soaking it in hot water. Or read Packing-Tape Transfers (pages 32–33) for another technique that works with some bottles. Don't worry if the labels don't come off perfectly. I think imperfection adds to their charm.

Here's the beginning of a list of items that are inexpensive and fun to buy. What can you think of to add to it?

- Postcards—They're wonderful for hard-to-photograph areas and great to journal on and include in your Scrapbook on the Go, or mail them home to yourself and assemble them into a book after you get home (see *Wish You Were Here* Scrapbook on the Go on page 60).

- Hat pins, tie tacks

- Souvenir patches

- Key chains—Keep these inexpensive souvenirs intact and attach them to your Scrapbook on the Go, or disassemble them and collage the parts onto your scrapbook spread

- Decks of cards with locations featured on the back—Keep the deck intact for playing on the road, and use the souvenir side of a joker to decorate one of your Scrapbook on the Go pages.

- Charms specific to the event or location

- Parking tokens or coins (especially foreign currency)

- Stickers specific to the location

Use pliers or a rock to flatten the edges of bottle caps that you want to be flat inside your book.

- Souvenir pressed pennies—you know, those kitschy pennies that come out impressed with a scene or feature unique to a place

- Beads or buttons from a shop you just happened to pass by

- A small piece of fabric or special yarn from a quilt store or yarn shop

If you're like other fabric and yarn collectors (including me!), you really don't need more; however, a special piece bought on the trip specifically for your scrapbook will always be special. Use some of it in your book that evening, and you'll still have some to take home and add to your stash for future projects.

How to Stay Organized

I hope your brain is full of ideas right now and you're really looking forward to your next Scrapbook on the Go opportunity. Now that you're thinking about the possibilities involved in making your Scrapbook on the Go, you'll need some ideas to help you stay organized away from home. Some of these methods require advance planning, and others rely on finds during your travels.

Option #1

Bring along an envelope, paper bag, or resealable plastic bag for each day of your trip. Everything from each day goes in its own envelope or bag until you have time to scrapbook it.

 An added advantage of this system: if you run out of time or lose interest in your scrapbook, you already have your items organized and together. Simply add your photographs to the envelopes or bags; then bind them together and tell people it was your intention all along! Be sure to check out *Brown Baggin' It* on page 54 and *On-the-Edge Envelope Book* on page 56 to give you even more quick and easy ideas.

Option #2

If you know you'll be shopping when you're away, use a shopping bag from that day's excursion to keep your collection safe instead of bringing bags from home.

 Whether you use envelopes or bags, new or recycled, bring a permanent marker to write on the outside of the bag. Include the date, where you went that day, what you did, who you saw, and a funny thing that happened or that someone said. Believe me, you won't remember details if you don't write them down, and you'll appreciate the memory jog when you are working on your Scrapbook on the Go.

Including a variety of envelopes and bags helps you stay organized.

finding time to scrapbook on the go

Great Ideas So Far, but How Do I Do This?

I'm married to the world champion "see everything you possibly can in the amount of time we have" man. Believe me, you don't want to get caught spending all your time scrapbooking and not experiencing the place or event! So, when can you find the time to Scrapbook on the Go?

SCENARIO 1: MORNINGS

Are you a morning person? Perhaps you're traveling with someone who likes to sleep in a bit longer than you do. Great! Get up at your normal time, and use 30 minutes or so of that quiet to arrange your ephemera. If you have any heavy items, glue them down during the last few minutes, and then head out for your day's adventure while the adhesive dries.

SCENARIO 2: IN THE CAR

I've been known to play in my book-in-progress while riding in a car. If you are using a glue stick or tape, it's easy to cut or tear your items and then paste or tape them into your Scrapbook on the Go while someone else is driving. Just wait for a stretch of smooth road to add your handwritten journaling. At the next stop, discard the remnants of your mini scrapbook session, and you're ready for the next adventure.

SCENARIO 3: EVENINGS

Are you a night person? After a full day of sightseeing and dinner, everyone is probably ready to relax. Join them! Relax at a small table with your collection from the day. Some people in my family like to watch TV in the evening. If you're sharing a hotel room or cabin, you're watching TV, too. Take advantage of that time to work in your scrapbook. It is the perfect time to journal about the day while everything is fresh in your mind.

Tip If you're not sure where on a spread you want the journaling, write on a separate piece of paper. Adhere the journaling to the page after you've placed all your photos and ephemera.

SCENARIO 4: INVOLVING OTHERS

Share the fun and speed the Scrapbook on the Go process at the same time. Get your family, friends, and other traveling companions in on the fun as you create. While you sort and arrange your ephemera and photos, have other people journal on some of the small pieces of paper you brought in your Scrapbook on the Go kit; then arrange it all to your satisfaction.

Let your kids have some input on how to arrange the stuff they collected that day. The scrapbook may not look exactly like it would if you'd done it by yourself, but it will hold very special meaning and memories for everyone who helped create it. And, after all, isn't the preservation of memories the real reason we scrapbook?

SCENARIO 5: LEAVING SPACES TO ADD PHOTOGRAPHS LATER

Sometimes I arrange the ephemera from the day on a spread and intentionally leave open spots where I would like to place my photos once I get them developed. This is a great way to speed up your Scrapbook on the Go project. After you've found a photo developer on the trip or have had your photographs processed at home, you'll need only a few minutes to place your pictures in your book. Your scrapbook will be finished before you know it! Don't worry about leaving exactly the right size area for your photographs. Overlapping items adds interest to pages.

SCENARIO 6: USING YOUR LUNCH HOUR

If you're getting your photos developed at a one-hour processor when traveling, drop them off before lunch. Enjoy your lunch break, pick the pictures up after lunch, and you won't have missed a minute of sightseeing opportunities.

SCENARIO 7: BOWING OUT

Be honest: Are you always interested in the same things as your traveling companions? Me neither. It's all right to say, "No thanks, you go ahead. I'll sit this one out." You might even consider scheduling activities for the others that you know they'll enjoy much more than you would. Find a historical site or a military museum on your route, or suggest that your companions go fishing for a few hours or maybe take a little detour to an amusement park. Thinking of what others might enjoy doing not only will make you look like a selfless person but also will create an opportunity for you to bow out and work in your Scrapbook on the Go. Everyone will be happy. They won't have to listen to you complain about not having a good time, and you will have some time to create and play in your Scrapbook on the Go. Win-win!

SCENARIO 8:
MAKING THE MOST OF DINNERTIME

If you're traveling with a digital camera and a portable photo printer, review the photographs on your memory card before dinner. Select the ones you want to print. Then, before you head out to eat, simply put the memory card into the slot and get the printer going. Make sure you've loaded enough photo paper into the printer. Your photos will be ready for you to scrapbook as soon as you get back from a relaxing dinner. Printing out photos doesn't have to be hard. Sometimes we just make it that way.

SCENARIO 9: TRAVELING BY PLANE

When faced with a long flight, I make the most of the time by finishing any remaining pages from the trip. Because you kept your ephemera organized by day (see How to Stay Organized, page 12), you don't need to have everything out at once. Simply get out your scrapbook, one day's collection, and a few embellishments. As you cut and paste, you'll realize that even the airplane pull-down tray is large enough for most projects. Your Scrapbook on the Go will be ready to share with family and friends as soon as you finish taxiing down the runway.

SCENARIO 10: LIMITING YOUR TIME

You might be thinking, "I work slowly." Perhaps you routinely spend more than 30 minutes on a scrapbook page or spread. Sometimes that's great. I'd like to challenge you, though, to try working more quickly. You've probably heard the saying of British scholar C. Northcote Parkinson: "Work expands so as to fill the time available for its completion." You know this is so true! Challenge yourself by setting a real or mental timer for less time than you think you'll need, and see what you can accomplish in your scrapbook during that time. Often, working spontaneously will result in a much more interesting layout than you would end up with for a carefully planned piece. Challenge yourself to glue down the first version of the page that looks good to you, and stop striving for the "perfect" layout. I sincerely believe that finished is better than perfect. Try it!

Can you think of any other times to squeeze in a few minutes to Scrapbook on the Go?

photography tips

This chapter presents some general photography tips that might improve the quality of the photographs you take for your Scrapbook on the Go. By no means are these tips meant to be all-inclusive. Of course, there are exceptions to almost all advice, but here are some general guidelines for improving your photographs.

- Take extra film, batteries, or memory cards with you when traveling.

- If your camera has a self-timer, use it to include yourself in photographs. Use a tripod or other means of supporting your camera.

Use the self-timer when no one is around to take your photo for you.

- Try not to cut people off at the knees when you photograph them.

- Know your flash range—don't use it to try to illuminate something too far away.

- Lighting is especially important when you are photographing people. Have people remove their hats, and keep them away from shadows. Don't let a person cast a shadow on another person's face when you are photographing them. If you can't avoid some shadows, use your camera's fill flash to illuminate the faces.

- Look your subject in the eye—get down at the subject's eye level for maximum impact.

Get down at your subject's eye level.

- Take some photographs in portrait (vertical) mode and some in landscape (horizontal) mode for variety. Try not to always center your subject in your photographs.

Photo by Tom Smiley

Photo by Tom Smiley

Vary the orientation of your photographs for interest. Slightly tilting a photo can be really cool, too.

- Take photos even in bad weather—rain or fog can make lighting appear more even (no shadows!) and colors seem brighter. Try to include a spot of color for extra interest.

This photo from Schwartz Bay looks wonderful, even though the day was foggy.

- Use the special features of your digital camera—sepia, black and white, and so on—for variety in your photographs.

Your camera's extra features add variety to your Scrapbook on the Go.

- Catch the action in photos for your Scrapbook on the Go.

Include action shots.

- Pay attention to the time of day. Morning and evening light are often the best for scenic photos. The colors appear richer.

Evening light makes photos rich.

- Use the panoramic mode on your camera if you have it.

- Tell a story with your photos. For example, take photos of people packing, leaving, and arriving at their destination; people engaged in activities during the day; and sleepy people on the way home. Print them smaller, and include them all on a Scrapbook on the Go spread.

- Shoot interesting and varied angles.

Pay attention to interesting angles to vary your photographs.

- Include people in your photographs to show scale.

Including people in scenic photographs lends a sense of scale.

- Last, but certainly not least, if you use a digital camera, get to know your photo-editing software. Use it to enhance, alter, and edit your photos. Adjust color, eliminate red-eye, remove something from the background, crop in on the subject, or even improve brightness and contrast.

Most of all, have fun, and remember to take lots of pictures!

paper pizzazz

Technique: Paper Backgrounds

Wow! The variety of scrapbooks and scrapbook papers from which to choose is amazing. Manufacturers continue to tempt us with scrapbooks in different sizes, shapes, and decorative covers. My advice when shopping for a scrapbook to use on the go is to buy a size that you will feel comfortable taking with you. Save the 12″ × 12″ size to work in when you are at home. I find that the 8″ × 8″ and 6″ × 6″ sizes are very portable and work well for my Scrapbook on the Go projects. Clear page-protector sleeves make it easy to work on one page or spread at a time; you can simply slide the finished page into your book, and you are ready to start the next page or to head out for your days' adventure.

PERSONALIZING SCRAPBOOK PAPER

Most scrapbooks come with plain white paper pages in the sleeves. If you're like me, you probably aren't thrilled with the idea of using plain white pages throughout your entire book. I like to add a splash of color to those pages with some paint or stamp some background images on them to bypass the dreaded "blank page syndrome."

If you have plain paper on hand, consider painting your own paper and then cutting it to fit your scrapbook, or simply paint the pages that came with your scrapbook. Use C&T's *Paper Crafter's Color Companion* (see Sources on page 63) to assist you in choosing paint colors. Easy Painted Backgrounds on page 23 will help you get started.

If you are not interested in painting paper, a visit to your local scrapbook or craft store will make your head reel. So many gorgeous scrapbook papers are now available that I always want to use as many as possible! I used a collection of papers from The Paper Loft (see Sources on page 63) for most of my *Far East Fascination* Scrapbook on the Go (see page 19).

A LITTLE PREPARATION GOES A LONG WAY

When you use a scrapbook with clear sleeves for your Scrapbook on the Go, I suggest cutting your background papers to size *before* the event or trip. Doing so makes it easier to transport your papers without damaging them and eliminates the need for precise cutting tools while away from home.

Use the theme of the event or the idea of the place you'll be traveling to as inspiration when choosing scrapbook papers. If you are not confident about your color sense, make this process easy on yourself by buying a prepackaged collection of coordinated papers. A designer has already done the work for you!

Tip

To boost your color confidence, try C&T's *Paper Crafter's Color Companion.*

The *Paper Crafter's Color Companion* will help you choose pleasing colors for your next Scrapbook on the Go.

Inspiration: Far East Fascination

WHAT I USED
Before I Left Home

- A blank scrapbook with clear page protectors

- A variety of papers, some plain and some from The Paper Loft, cut to fit inside the page sleeves

- An inside "title page" decorated with the names of the places we were traveling to and the dates

- Travel words printed with my label maker

- Film negative strips gathered from that drawer or shoebox full of old negatives that most of us have

On the Road

- A digital camera (I use photo labs and self-serve photo-processing machines in my destination cities.)

- Paper tags from The Paper Loft and BasicGrey collections (see Sources on page 63)

- Tape

- Scissors

- A glue stick

- Pens for journaling

- Ephemera collected on the journey

Tip

Cardstock is great for scrapbook backgrounds. The extra weight of the paper helps support embellishments, paints, found objects, and so on.

PAPER PIZZAZZ PLUS!

Found papers, such as shopping bags, brochures, maps, and the like, that you collect along the way can be wonderful backgrounds for your Scrapbook on the Go. These papers generally will not be archival, so keep that in mind if that issue is important to you.

Slip-out pages make it easy to Scrapbook on the Go, as shown by this spread I made on my fold-down tray on the airplane flight. Most of the words and images, including the map, came from the free in-flight magazine. I added the Singapore flag sticker and the airplane photo later.

I like to start my first page or spread before I leave home. Using paper and red mesh tape, I simply printed the words on my computer and added some metal embellishments to set the tone for the book. The blue paper was the result of using a paper punch. Instead of using the squares, I used the negative shapes as frames around my words.

Before you leave home, use dabbing, dry-brush, or direct-to-paper techniques with your stamp pads to add color to your background papers. For this spread, I used tags, Singapore flea market finds, index prints, names of places cut from local maps and brochures, and photo negative strips (from my Scrapbook on the Go kit) to complete this spread in my hotel room at the end of the day.

Combine different textures of paper for a spread. These two pages are very similar colors, but the different textures add interest. The coaster and bamboo fruit skewers from the world-famous Singapore Slings just had to be included in my Scrapbook on the Go!

Be open to using found or newly acquired papers along the way. Although I had precut paper for my Scrapbook on the Go before leaving home, I decided that the map from the Singapore Zoo would make a wonderful background for some of the photos I took that day.

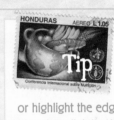

Use the paper just as you bought it, or highlight the edges by rubbing them lightly with a stamp pad, a little bit of paint on a sponge, or the tip of a Copic marker (see Sources on page 63) to add your unique touch.

The green background on this spread was a paper bag from a photo-processing shop in Singapore. I added some stamped images and a few found objects from the produce market and stapled on my journaling to complete this simple spread.

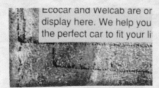

Highlight the edge of your scrapbook paper with a stamp pad to add depth of color, additional interest, and a personal touch to your project.

Note

The variety of scrapbook papers available for purchase is absolutely incredible. If you can think of it, it's probably already out there waiting for you to buy it. New scrapbook stores are opening up every day, but you can also shop at craft stores or online. See Sources on page 63 for some of my favorite paper companies.

Backgrounds don't always need to be made of paper. I found this wonderful Japanese Yukata fabric in a small shopping area and couldn't resist buying a few small pieces. I gently frayed the edges and layered my photographs on top.

Capture a Sense of Place

Sometimes we want our scrapbook pages to convey the energy of a place. Tokyo is a bustling city, and I wanted to express that energy by creating a very busy spread in my Scrapbook on the Go. Photos, receipts, tape, labels, and ephemera all contribute to the hectic feeling. See if you can capture a place in your next scrapbook spread.

Include Details

Because I was working on my Scrapbook on the Go during the trip, why not include that process in my book? Mundane details really help you remember everything about the trip.

Take Advantage of Unexpected Finds

When we were in Tokyo, we visited the Toyota showroom. It had stations set up on each floor for kids to stamp little monkey images—a great idea, as it kept little ones busy looking for the stamping stations while their parents were looking at the new vehicles. Of course, I couldn't see rubber stamps without wanting to play, too! I cut out and added my stamped images to some negative strips from my Scrapbook on the Go kit.

When we were in the airport leaving Tokyo, the tourism bureau was doing a survey. We had a few extra minutes, so I politely answered questions. When I was finished, the lovely interviewer handed me a gorgeous package of origami papers. I included these totally unexpected and very appreciated mementoes in my Scrapbook on the Go as I worked on these last few pages on the flight home.

Wrap It Up

It's always fun to have a final page that brings the trip, and your project, to a close. I used the "solarize" option on my digital camera to take this photo from the airplane on the flight back to the United States. I did the hand stitches after we got home, and my Scrapbook on the Go was ready to share.

A variety of
paints and inks

paint play

Technique: Easy Painted Backgrounds

Even those of us who have no prior experience with paints can successfully create wonderful painted backgrounds for our work. Here are a few super simple steps for creating great colored backgrounds in your Scrapbook on the Go. I love doing this phase of my Scrapbook on the Go ahead of time on plain cardstock or, better yet, in a blank board book (see Sources, page 63). Completing the backgrounds before the trip or event saves you the trouble of packing paints, worrying about leakage, and needing to be extremely cautious with paints in a hotel room.

Give it a try. Believe me, you can paint interesting backgrounds. They are simple, easy, fast, and incredibly fun to do. Create backgrounds that are uniquely yours in four steps or less. Be bold: read on!

Think ahead about your trip or the event that you plan to scrapbook. If you are planning a trip, look at your itinerary. What's the first color you think of when you envision your destination or activity?

Try it: The beach? Sand and blue for water. The woods? A variety of greens, and maybe some tan and brown for the forest floor. A party? Hot, fun colors like fuchsia, orange, or turquoise.

Use your initial color idea as you gather paints, inks, and stamp pads that are close to belonging in that color family. Say, for example, that you want a green background for your Scrapbook on the Go. Get out your yellow-green stamp pad, your blue-green paint, and your olive green ink. If you don't have a wide variety of colors, it's no big deal. Mix the ones you do have in varying amounts to make a variety of tints and shades. Plain white cardstock and blank board books are both ready to accept paint right out of the jar or tube; no prep work is necessary, so let's get to it.

Creating Easy Painted Backgrounds

1. Use a foam brush to apply the dominant color paint or ink to your page or spread. Don't fixate on even or thorough paint coverage; just get some color onto most of the page. If you want to color the edges of your pages, feel free to do that at any time with any of your related colors. Allow the paint to dry.

Painting the base color

2. Place a few drops of each of your related ink or paint colors onto a clean lid or palette. Use a color related to your base color, or highlight using a complementary color.

3. With a clean cosmetic sponge, pick up a bit of each of your ink colors, and dab them onto the painted page. Use the side of the cosmetic sponge to spread the inks all around on the page. Allow the ink to dry.

Adding inks

Don't have inks? Thin your acrylic paint with glazing medium, which stretches the color and makes it somewhat translucent.

4. Rub your stamp pad over the dry page to highlight some areas and give it texture. Use one stamp pad, or more if you have appropriate colors. Let it dry.

Direct application of ink to page with stamp pads

5. Use a stamp pad or some ink on your gloved finger to highlight the edges of the page. I like to use at least one shade darker here. Or try using a complementary color to add some extra punch to your board book page. Allow it to dry thoroughly, and heat set it if any of the products you used require it.

See how easy and fun this is? I knew you could do it! Now let's take a look at my *California Here We Come* Scrapbook on the Go, where I followed these exact steps when preparing my blank board book for the trip.

WHAT YOU'LL NEED

- Rubber gloves—the inexpensive, disposable ones work well
- A foam brush—1″ or 2″ wide are the most versatile
- A cosmetic sponge—the wedge-shaped ones are great
- A newspaper, vinyl tablecloth, or old catalog to protect your work surface
- A variety of acrylic paints, dye inks, calligraphy inks, stamp pads, and so on
- Some type of palette for your paints

A clean plastic lid from food containers makes an excellent disposable tray for mixing colors.

WHAT I USED

Before I Left Home

- An 8″ × 8″ blank board book from C&T Publishing

- Jo Sonja acrylic paints

- Foam paintbrushes

I used the easy techniques just described to create the backgrounds in my blank board book before the trip began.

On the Road

- An 8″ × 8″ blank board book with painted backgrounds (see Easy Painted Backgrounds on pages 23–24)

- A digital camera and portable color printer (or print your photos at places along the way)

- A rubber stamp alphabet and black stamp pad

- Scissors

- Nexus pens for journaling

- A glue stick for paper items

- The Ultimate! adhesive for heavy items (see Sources, page 63)

- Ephemera, maps, shells, feathers, and other found objects collected on the trip

I painted this background a blue-green color, knowing we would be flying over the San Francisco Bay and heading to Muir Woods, north of the city. Ticket stubs, a park brochure, a coffee cozy, business cards, and found objects were arranged to complete this first spread on the trip. I turned an REI freebie into a fold-down pocket that holds more photos from the day and handwrote my journaling with a favorite pen.

When I think of the San Francisco Bay, I think of fog and cool weather. I translated those thoughts into gray and foggy turquoise paints that I used to paint this background. The Golden Gate postcard holder (bought on clearance at the park store) became a pocket to hold the day's photographs. Notice the stamps from the national park and the lighthouse association. Part of another coffee cozy, the ferry schedule, ticket stubs, and fragments of paper bags were some of the other collage items available to me at the end of the day. I journaled with a pen and also with my rubber stamp set, playing off a popular commercial about what's priceless in life.

Rather than include an entire cork in your book, which would cause the book to warp, use a craft knife to cut a sliver from the side of the cork. Try to include the name or artwork in your fragment to help you recall the time and place. I can still picture the outdoor seating area with our table next to the fireplace at the restaurant where I collected this cork.

Driving down the coast of California. I knew we'd see a lot of the Pacific Ocean, so I used a deep rich teal for this day's background. Photos from the aquarium, part of a cork from a special bottle of wine at dinner, and a few other items collected from the day come together on this spread.

Another deep teal, watery background for this spread documenting another day on the Pacific coastline. Photographs, a flower petal, a flat rock, and a souvenir penny add some dimension to this spread. Even a photo of a highway marker sign that some might think mundane can be incorporated into your Scrapbook on the Go.

 Tip I filled the sand dollar on this spread with liquid adhesive. Once dry, the adhesive supports the shell from the inside, making it less likely to break. Use the same idea to support other 3-dimensional fragile items.

Farther south in California, temperatures rise. I carried this idea through by painting the background a warm color. Seashells, feathers, fallen bark, and paper ephemera all support the handwritten journaling on this Scrapbook on the Go spread.

Use my painted background board book as inspiration for your next Scrapbook on the Go project. The sturdy pages create a wonderful base for 3-dimensional and other heavier items, including pockets full of photographs and ephemera. See Sources (page 63) for other board book sizes.

Paper bags make wonderful pockets for holding all the extras that we can't seem to part with. A highlighted map showing our route, the rest of the wine bottle cork, and part of a film wrapper decorate the bag, which is filled to overflowing with ephemera from our trip.

texture time

Technique: Textured Backgrounds

I love texture—the variety of textures on tree bark, the grainy texture of sand, the rough texture of burlap, the smooth texture of paper. I also love the visual texture of an intense colored background. I think it's the variety of texture that appeals to me as much as any one texture by itself.

We can create a textured background in many ways. Following up on the painted backgrounds we explored in the previous chapter, we could simply add texture medium to our paint to create easy textured backgrounds. We could use textured cloth or a variety of textured papers as backgrounds. How about creating an interesting textured background from a smooth paper? That sounds like fun!

WHAT YOU'LL NEED

- A blank or reclaimed board book—see *Altered Board Book Basics and Beyond* for detailed information about reclaiming board books (see Sources on page 63)

- Tan and green masking papers from the paint aisle at the home improvement store, which are inexpensive and come on a roll about 12″ wide

- The Ultimate! adhesive

- Optional—a variety of colored tapes (electrical tape, masking tape, and tapes from the art supply store)

CREATING TEXTURED BACKGROUNDS

1. Tear or cut a piece of masking paper a couple of inches larger on each side than your book spread.

2. Crumple the paper up in your hand as if you were going to throw it away.

3. Open the paper back up again, but do not smooth it out.

4. Crumple the paper a second time.

5. Open up the paper, smoothing it just slightly.

6. Use an old credit card or hotel key card to spread a thin layer of The Ultimate! adhesive all over your book spread.

 I prefer to use The Ultimate! for this step, as it creates a stronger bond between the masking paper and the board book than most glue sticks do.

7. Gently lay your crinkled masking paper on top of the adhesive, keeping some wrinkles intact. Don't try to smooth all the wrinkles out, or you'll lose the wonderful texture.

8. After the adhesive is dry, use the edge of the board book page as your cutting guide, and carefully trim away the excess masking paper. Use a craft knife, rotary cutter, or scissors.

9. Repeat this process for each spread, alternating green and tan backgrounds.

Optional: Add tape around the edges of the pages.

 Electrical tape stretches, so it makes a great edge for the rounded corners of some board books. Simply stretch it a little bit as you cover the edges of the book. Don't obsess about getting it exactly straight on both sides of the page. I think any irregularity of the tape line adds to the charm of the book.

Cool, isn't it? It's simple, inexpensive, and ready for your Scrapbook on the Go.

 Look for other papers to use for this technique. I've used paper from the art supply store, architects' sketch paper, and art tissue papers. Be wary of paper with a very slick surface, as it will resist most adhesives. If a paper you love doesn't like glue, try using brads, eyelets, and hand stitching to hold items in place in your Scrapbook on the Go.

 To accentuate the texture of these backgrounds even more, lightly rub a stamp pad across the surface. The higher areas of the paper will pick up color and enhance the look.

Inspiration: Colorado Mountain Adventure

WHAT I USED
Before I Left Home

- 3 blank or reclaimed board books—see *Altered Board Book Basics and Beyond* for information on reclaiming board books (see Sources on page 63)
- Masking paper
- Electrical tape
- The Ultimate! adhesive

Using the technique just described for creating textured backgrounds, I glued all the textured background papers and applied various tapes to the book prior to our trip. I reclaimed a tall, narrow children's board book and a small children's board book, plus one 3″ × 3″ blank board book from C&T Publishing. After covering the little books with paper and tape, I used The Ultimate! adhesive to adhere them to the front of the larger book.

On the Road

- Board books with textured paper backgrounds and taped edges
- A digital camera and photo printer
- A tiny bag with a variety of ribbons, brads, tags, and embellishments
- Small pieces of lined paper for journaling
- Scissors
- A glue stick
- The Ultimate! adhesive for heavier items

The front cover of my Colorado Mountain Adventure *Scrapbook on the Go*. I thought that the two little books adhered to the front of this scrapbook would give me an interesting place to include smaller items and to decorate some miniature spreads. The Colorado postage stamp decorates the cover, along with words from travel brochures, a family photo we took early in the trip, and a couple of embellishments from my Scrapbook on the Go kit. A close-up of our family photo from Rocky Mountain National Park illustrates how a simple photograph and a small amount of ribbon can be all a cover needs to be complete.

No matter how good a photographer you are, there will be days when your photos don't turn out the way you want them to. Or perhaps you are participating in an activity where you don't want to risk having your camera along. What can you do to document these kinds of days? Use a brochure! Travel brochures are a wonderful source of photographs, words, and details about many activities and places.

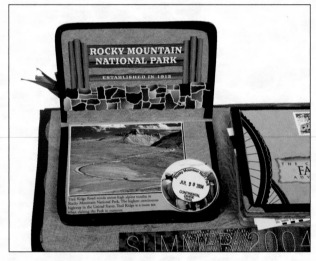

This miniature spread includes Rocky Mountain stickers found at a shop on the trip, a National Parks Passport stamp, and a hard-to-photograph scene from a national park brochure.

We loved Boulder! Using a couple of embellishments from my kit, part of the downtown map (which helps us remember restaurant and shop names), and souvenirs of our tea tour, I quickly finished this simple spread.

Tip

Layering the books together was a lot of fun. It was a challenge to find items small enough to include in the minibooks, but I like the cover a lot. Try mixing sizes of books and colors of backgrounds for an upcoming Scrapbook on the Go project of your own.

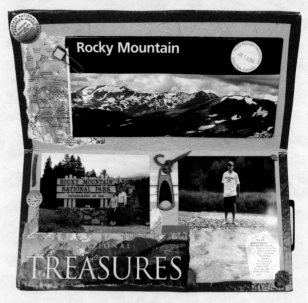

For this spread, I gleaned images and words from local travel and business freebies. I journaled on the lined papers I had in my *Scrapbook on the Go* kit. Torn into small pieces, these bits can be used to fill in gaps between collage elements. An inexpensive souvenir pin and some found objects complete the spread.

Rocky Mountain National Park had so much to offer: hikes, beautiful vistas, cold streams, and family. A park map, brochure, and photographs made this an easy spread to complete.

A busier spread, but still easy to complete using group and individual photographs layered with maps, postcards, coffee cozy parts, and journaling. The bands at the top and bottom are reminders of my trips to the health clinic while on the trip. They are not fun to remember but were definitely a part of the trip!

Part of a travel magazine yielded the perfect image and words to cover the large envelope in the back of my Colorado Mountain Adventure *Scrapbook on the Go*. I simply glued the magazine page to the front of the envelope, added some hand-dyed twill tape from Scenic Route Paper Co. to reinforce the envelope opening, and put all the remaining brochures and photographs inside. The vintage tab was a bonus find when I got home to my studio. Similar reproduction label holders are available at scrapbook stores.

This page from my *Far East Fascination* Scrapbook on the Go has a packing-tape transfer border. The beads were from a magazine ad.

Sticky fingers

Technique:
Packing-Tape Transfers

Here's a fast, fun, inexpensive, and easy process to use in your Scrapbook on the Go. These low-tech transfers are easy to do and slightly addictive once you get started. They are also easy enough for kids to do.

WHY DO PACKING-TAPE TRANSFERS?

This transfer method results in an image that you can partially see through. Think titles for your Scrapbook on the Go pages or layering of text and images. This is just another cool technique you'll want to incorporate into many of your projects.

Tip Don't use your fingernails to rub during any part of this process unless you intend to scratch part of the image off the tape.

WHAT YOU'LL NEED

- Clear packing tape—the inexpensive kind is fine
- An image or text cut or torn from a magazine, brochure, or calendar page
- A container large enough to hold your image
- A large spoon or bone folder (helpful but not essential)
- Warm water

MAKING PACKING-TAPE TRANSFERS

1. Tear or cut your image from the rest of the page.

2. Place the image right side up on a firm, flat surface.

3. Cover the image with clear packing tape. If the image is wider than the tape, overlap the edges of the tape slightly until the entire image is covered.

4. Use the back of a spoon, a bone folder, or the palm of your hand to ensure that the packing tape is firmly bonded to the image. Check from the right side of the image, and burnish any air bubbles or areas that don't look firmly attached.

5. Place the taped image in a container of warm water, and let it soak for 5 to 10 minutes.

6. Remove the taped image from the water, and use your thumb to rub the back side of the image. The paper will start to roll off, leaving just the ink and the clear tape.

7. Continue to rub gently until you have removed as much of the paper as possible.

 If your tape still has paper residue left on it after drying, soak and gently rub it again to remove the residue.

 Throw the paper that rubbed off the back of the image in the trash. Do not put it down the drain, as it will contribute to clogs in the pipes.

8. Set the image and tape aside for a couple of minutes to dry.

9. Attach the tape and image to your Scrapbook on the Go page. The tape might not be sticky enough to stay on your page. If this is so, use a light hand with a glue stick or clear gel medium to adhere the tape to your page. Other options for attaching it to your page include staples, clips, or brads.

Inspiration: Packing-Tape Transfers in Use

 If you find yourself making all kinds of packing-tape transfers (I warned you that they are slightly addictive), store them in clear page protectors to keep them from sticking together until you are ready to use them.

An image from a college magazine was cut to fit the front of an envelope inside the back cover of the College Search book. Overlapping the tape slightly allowed me to use this large image. I secured it around the edges with—what else—more tape. This envelope is ready for additional photos and brochures as we continue our quest for the right school.

I included a packing-tape transfer of a wine bottle label on this spread in my journal. Notice the masking tape hinge I used on the right-hand page to layer a postcard and bookmark while retaining access to the journal page behind it.

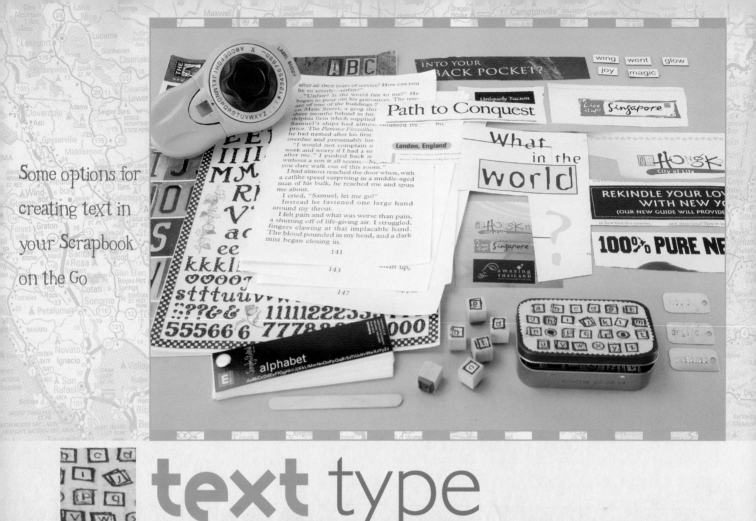

Some options for creating text in your Scrapbook on the Go

 text type

Technique: Getting Text Onto Your Scrapbook on the Go Pages

No matter what event or trip you are commemorating, chances are pretty good that you are going to want to incorporate *some* text on your pages. Let's explore fun ways to say what you need to say. You'll see most of these ideas incorporated into my Scrapbook on the Go projects throughout this book.

Option 1 One obvious way to get text onto your Scrapbook on the Go page is to grab a pen, pencil, or marker and write. Even if you hate your handwriting, be sure to include *some* handwritten text. It's your handwriting that will make your Scrapbook on the Go unique to *you* and very special to your family for years to come. For added variety and a fun brainteaser, try using your nondominant hand to write a few words or a title.

Tip
A recycled mint tin is perfect for housing alphabet stamps!

Tip
Do you really want to include journaling in your Scrapbook on the Go but don't want everyone to be able to read your innermost thoughts? Try journaling on a tag that you tuck into a pocket or envelope. How about using a pen color that doesn't contrast much with your paper color, so the viewer has to get up close to read it? How about journaling on the back of a piece of collage ephemera and attaching it on just one side, so the viewer has to turn it over to read it? How about journaling around the edges of your page or a tag, so viewers have to turn the whole book to read it, making it less likely they will do so? How about journaling underneath a photograph that's only attached by photo corners? You'll know it's there, but no one else will. See how sneaky you can be in including, but also protecting, your private thoughts.

Option 2 Have your significant other, your friends, or your kids journal onto your scrapbook pages. If you don't want them writing directly on your pages, have them write on another piece of cut or torn paper, and then glue or tape that piece of paper into your book.

Option 3 Some spreads might look great with computer-generated text. Don't let that stop you from working on your visual Scrapbook on the Go while you're away. Take the time to write down the words you want to use on each page. After you get home, type up the text, print it out, and glue it in your book to complete your spread.

Option 4 Add a label maker to your Scrapbook on the Go kit, and use it to add words to your spread. This idea works especially well for titles, city names, key words, and so on. Or print out some words before you leave home, and add them to your kit.

Option 5 Cut or tear words from magazines, travel brochures, or literature you picked up at the hotel, in a restaurant, or on the subway. A quick session with your glue stick, and you'll have the text just where you want it on your page.

Option 6 Buy large-print books at tag sales or used bookstores. Add a few pages to your Scrapbook on the Go kit, cut the easy-to-read words from them, and then simply glue the text onto your scrapbook page.

Option 7 Rubber stamp alphabets are fun to use and readily available in hundreds of fonts and sizes. If you aren't comfortable stamping directly on your page, stamp onto another piece of cut or torn paper, and then glue or tape that piece of paper onto your page. Choose a small or unmounted stamp set for ease

of travel. Save your larger, heavier sets for adding titles once you're back home. Rubber stamp words are available, too.

Option 8 Use stickers and rub-ons to add text to your pages. You can purchase alphabets in different fonts and colors, as well as words and phrases, at craft stores, scrapbook stores, and office supply stores.

Option 9 Magnetic poetry words or dog tag words can be great sources of text for your scrapbook pages, too. Simply add a brad or eyelet, and you're ready for the next page.

Option 10 Put an old typewriter back into commission. If you don't have one in a closet somewhere, ask family members, or look for one at yard sales, thrift stores, or flea markets. Clean it up, replace the ribbon if it needs it, and type your text. Type onto lightweight paper, cut or tear it apart, and then collage the bits of typewritten text onto your spread. I know you're not going to carry a typewriter with you when you travel, but if you think ahead and type a page of words, names, appropriate phrases, and action words, the single sheet of paper will take up practically no space in your kit and can hold *a lot* of text for you to cut apart and use in your Scrapbook on the Go.

Throughout this book, you'll see lots of examples of these ideas in my scrapbooks. Look and figure out what will work best for you in your next Scrapbook on the Go.

Do you have so much journaling that you're having trouble fitting it all on the page? Cut the journaling into several sections, and spread them around the page for added visual interest. Go ahead and overlap the journaling with the collaged ephemera to hold everything together visually.

When you include text on separate pieces of paper, highlight the edges with a small stamp pad or a Copic marker to help it stand out from the rest of your collaged items.

I find brads easier to use than eyelets when I Scrapbook on the Go. They don't require any special tools to use successfully. I use eyelets more when I'm at home with all my tools on hand.

Inspiration: Victorian Delight

WHAT I USED
Before I Left Home

- A scrapbook kit from Making Memories (I purchased 3 kraft color sections: pockets, envelope, and covers.)
- Fresco chalk inks in blues and greens (You could use acrylic paint, too.)
- A foam paintbrush
- A water pattern rubber stamp from Stampscapes
- A Fiskars grid brayer
- Scrapbook papers

Although I loved the minibook kit I bought, I wanted to add color and texture to the plain kraft background. I was heading to Victoria (an island city) and Vancouver (a coastal city), in British Columbia, so I immediately thought of water and evergreen trees. Using this idea, I stamped the outer covers with a water pattern rubber stamp and then brushed green ink over that for an extra bit of color. For the inner pages and large square tags inside the pockets, I used these same inks and a brayer with a grid pattern, which added color and visual texture while leaving the background paper still visible. For additional variety, I glued scrapbook paper pieces to parts of some pages.

My book had background color, as well as some visual texture, and was ready to head to the airport with me for my Scrapbook on the Go adventure.

A brochure I found early in the trip gave me the perfect title for my book. The colors were great, and the size was perfect. A bottle cap found several days into the trip was secured in place with The Ultimate! adhesive.

On the Road

- A stamped and painted scrapbook kit from Making Memories, plus the painted tags for inside some of the pockets
- A digital camera (I used photo-processing stores to print my photos on the trip.)
- Nexus pens for journaling
- 2 or 3 Copic markers for coloring and highlighting found papers
- Rub-on alphabets from Making Memories
- Embellishments from ARTchix Studio
- Blue cloth tarp repair tape (or other colored tape)
- A glue stick
- Scissors
- The Ultimate! adhesive for heavier items
- A few brads, clips, and other embellishments
- Ephemera, found objects, and inexpensive purchases along the way

Although I colored and arranged the book parts before the trip, I did not bind the book together until after I returned home. This technique allowed me the flexibility of working with individual parts of the book when arranging, gluing, and fastening items to the pages.

Tip

Tearing instead of cutting paper and using a glue stick or tape allow you to work safely in your Scrapbook on the Go while someone else is driving. Don't forget to enjoy the view, but take advantage of these bits of time to capture the excitement and energy of recent events.

The inside title page was simple. I just tore the words from my map. The season was torn from another travel brochure. The found tab was fun to include and functions as a "page turner." I purchased the tiny embellishments from ARTchix Studio on the trip and simply glued them in place. The tag inside the pocket includes ticket receipts and a photo taken through the window of the plane before we changed flights.

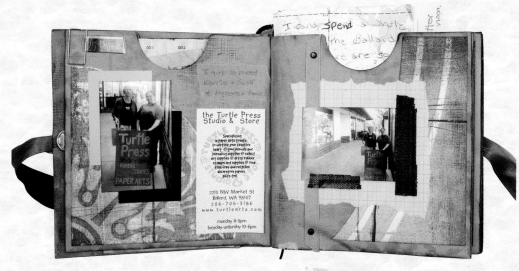

As we were driving north out of the Seattle airport, I somehow convinced my husband to stop at the Turtle Press store to shop and meet the wonderful owners, Kerrie and Scott. The great new ribbon, grid paper, and Nexus pen I bought, and even part of the paper bag, were all included when I arranged this quick spread.

A few photographs, the top ply of a buffet napkin, a sticker bought in the ship's gift shop, and journaling were all that I needed to complete this spread. I wanted to include the journaling but didn't want it to dominate the page, so I chose a low-contrast ink pen color.

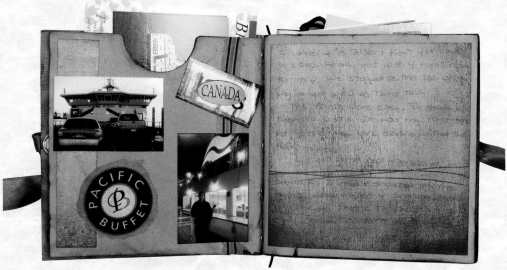

I don't usually throw away my photo fragments or ephemera until I'm done with my Scrapbook on the Go. Often these fragments will add just the right finishing touch to another spread. Using similar pieces throughout your book also helps to unify the pages.

A day spent walking around and browsing Victoria's business district. I found some great shops, which these pages reflect. I included the wonderful tissue paper, a round tag, parts of bags, a small piece of fabric from a quilt shop, a button from a wonderful button store, and the rest of the airplane from the photo on the inside title page. None of these items was expensive, but together they created new energy for this spread, and the leftovers became souvenirs to use in future projects.

If you've been looking at this book for more than a few minutes, you've probably noticed that I'm a coffee lover. I love finding locally owned or regional coffee shops when I travel, so I couldn't resist adding this coffee shop brochure to my Scrapbook on the Go.

Victoria's public art includes orcas decorated by many different artists. I tucked the orca-watching map (locations around town where the art is found) into the pocket behind this photo and continued to use the blue tape as both a decorative and functional element.

I used one of the large painted tags as a background on this page, along with another small piece of the fabric from the quilt shop. The "Explore" stamp is one of my hand-carved stamps. Notice the cropped photo of the light-house stairway, the small pebbles collected from that beach, and the pin purchased at the gift shop. The brick is a leftover part of another photograph.

When you have your digital photos printed, print them at different sizes. The harbor photo on this spread is a wallet-size photo (about 2″ × 3″), with the white border left intact, whereas the piling and rope photo was printed a full 4″ × 6″ size. If you get thumbnails printed (20 or more images on a 4″ × 6″ piece of photo paper), they can be cut apart and used to enhance a spread or be used in a miniature Scrapbook on the Go.

Two photographs, a phrase from a local travel brochure, and some rub-on letters complete this calm spread. The background paper for the harbor photo was edged with a Copic marker so it wouldn't disappear into the page. The island time phrase was completely colored with a Copic marker so that its stark whiteness wouldn't dominate the spread. This spread also shows the center of the book and the knotted binding cord that I tied the book with after I returned home.

When buying tape to use as a decorative and functional element in your Scrapbook on the Go, look for tape that tears easily. Tearing the tape saves you lots of time and frustration in cutting small pieces and sometimes yields a nice torn edge. Usually you can't test tape to see how it tears before you buy it, but with experience you'll learn which tapes work best for your Scrapbook on the Go style.

I had a fabulous time tearing my tape into small pieces to use on this spread. A combination of wallet-size photos alongside a full 4″ × 6″ photo, rub-on letters, and a feather found on the rocky shore were all that I needed to commemorate a beautiful day.

Tip

Use detail photographs as a background for feature photos. I love to take close-up pictures of peeling paint, crumbling walls, and rusty metal.

My husband loves boats. Victoria has the coolest harbor ferry boats, so of course we went for a ride. I combined other boat photographs from the trip and some purchased trim "ribbon" that reminds me of boat nets. The sailboat photo folds down to reveal the harbor ferry brochure.

Remember what I said about not throwing away leftovers until your Scrapbook on the Go is complete? Well, this book wouldn't be complete until I signed it, so I used a leftover piece of the photograph from the center spread on the back cover to finish it off.

In Vancouver my friend Lelainia took me to some of her favorite shopping destinations. With a quick snapshot and a few business cards, I can remember all the highlights of our fun day.

Look for kits that allow you flexibility in the layout and number of pages for your next Scrapbook on the Go. You also don't need to settle for whatever color paper the kits come with. Add some paint, direct-to-paper techniques with your stamp pads, or scrapbook papers to personalize your book before you head out on your next adventure.

A peek inside the box draws you in to look at the treasures inside.

 # book-free zone

Technique: Not a Book at All

Even with the variety of scrapbooks on the market today, we don't have to make all of our Scrapbooks on the Go in book form. Think about using something a little different every once in a while to increase your enthusiasm for a new project.

How about recycling a beautiful cigar box? How about a decorative tin from chocolates or note cards? How about using a CD carrying case and making round Scrapbook on the Go pages? How about using loose tags and decorating a small tin to keep them safe? How about a papier-mâché box to hold your treasures?

These examples show thinking outside of the box—I mean, outside of the book. I hope they will encourage you to think of other interesting containers to use for future projects.

Shells and beach glass collected on various islands now shine in a jar next to my treasure chest.

Inspiration: Treasure Chest

WHAT I USED
Before I Left Home

- A papier-mâché treasure chest box from the craft store—a nice stiff container for keeping my papers, photos, and embellishments safe

- Scenic Route Paper Co. scrapbook papers (I cut a variety of these scrapbook papers to a size just slightly smaller than the inside of my papier-mâché treasure chest.)

An inexpensive papier-mâché box can be painted or collaged with papers to house your next Scrapbook on the Go. This one was quickly painted and sponged in watery blue tones to remind us of our Caribbean cruise. We collected the shells on the trip, and they seem just right next to the box.

On the Cruise

- A digital camera and portable printer

- Hand-dyed twill tape in a variety of colors from Scenic Route Paper Co. (see Sources, page 63)

- A journaling pen (I journaled on the back of the individual cards)

- Embellishments—brads, metal frames

- A glue stick

- Scissors

- Sticky Stax adhesive-backed solid color papers from Colorbök (see Sources, page 63)

- Luggage tags, key cards, and other ephemera collected on the trip

After I Got Home

I painted and sponged the box with Jo Sonja acrylic paints and added the rub-on words. I'm glad I didn't do this ahead of time, because the last cab driver smashed my suitcase in the trunk and broke the top of the box. I bought another one when I got home, and that's the one I painted.

Here are some completed "pages" from inside the box. When working with loose pages, you cannot obsess about the order of the images. Putting a date on each image allows you to rearrange them as you like. One thing I really like about this box of photos is that a lot of people can be looking at the "scrapbook" at the same time. No one has to wait for someone to turn the page to see what's next.

I couldn't resist this papier-mâché flip-flop. I lightly sponged it with the same acrylic paints as the larger box. It became the perfect place to keep a few 3-dimensional items collected on the trip, and it fits neatly inside the treasure chest box and helps prop up the photographs.

Inspiration: Tin Treasures

Recycle or buy a tin container to keep your Scrapbook on the Go safe and sound. I had several related photos from our day in Belize that I wanted to keep together. This tin was the perfect place to document the day spent traveling to the Mayan ruins, and it fits neatly inside the treasure chest box with the rest of the cruise photographs.

Using a brayer with a grid pattern and a light touch, I took some chalk inks and added color to the accordion paper that came inside the tin to eliminate the dreaded blank white page. I simply cropped the photos to an appropriate size, and my accordion Tin Treasures Scrapbook on the Go was complete.

aLL dried up

Technique: Drying Plant Material in Your Microwave

I love to collect plant material to include in my Scrapbook on the Go. Leaves from beneath the tree where you had a fun picnic, flower petals, leaves in pretty fall colors, seed pods, and even interesting parts of a weed can help you remember a special time or place.

Note

Be aware of local ordinances. Never pick rare or endangered plant material or any plant material inside a national park or other protected area. Look for fallen plant parts rather than picking fresh material.

Because we are making a Scrapbook on the Go, chances are we don't want to wait for the "use patience" method of drying our plant material inside a large book. Instead, we can use a microwave oven to help speed the drying process.

Note

Thoroughly clean the microwave after using it for this task. You never know what insecticides, herbicides, or other material may have been on that plant when you harvested it.

1. Harvest the plant material (leaves, stems, buds, seeds, or flowers). Use your fingers to gently flatten and arrange it.

2. Place the plant material between clean sheets of paper.

Note

If you use paper with text on it, the ink might transfer to your plant material.

3. Layer the plant material, sandwiched in paper, between multiple layers of clean paper towels, paper napkins, or additional layers of paper.

4. Place all of these layers underneath a heavy, flat, nonmetallic object. If you don't weigh it down, the plant material will curl up as it dries. Be creative when trying to find a heavy item to use. A small part of a concrete block, a ceramic coaster, or even a book can be used as a weight. Be sure the stack will lie flat inside the microwave.

5. Place this entire sandwich—layers of paper or paper towel, clean paper, plant material, another layer of clean paper, and another layer of paper or paper towel, topped with the heavy object—in the microwave.

6. Set the microwave on high for 1 minute. Depending on the number of items you are drying and their thickness, you may need more time.

7. Allow the plant material to cool before you decide if it needs more time in the microwave. Repeat the microwave process in 20-second increments until your plant material is completely dry. Let the items cool completely before putting them into your Scrapbook on the Go.

When adhering dried plant material to your Scrapbook on the Go, use gel medium-matte medium, semigloss medium, or gloss medium, depending on your desired finished look.

You can apply the gel medium directly to the back of your plant material, carefully using a foam brush and a light touch, or you can coat the entire page with the medium and then arrange the plant material on top of the page. Cover the plant material with waxed paper, and press to adhere it completely to the page.

Note

Microwave ovens perform at different rates. Be sure to check your plant material frequently, and be careful when removing the items from the microwave—they might be *hot!*

Inspiration: Using Plant and Other Natural Materials in Your Scrapbook on the Go

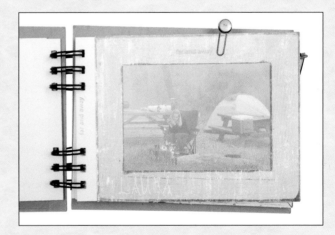

Did you think you couldn't make progress in your Scrapbook on the Go without electricity? Our Camping Book cover was decorated before the trip, but you could use dirt, soot from the campfire, berries, or even grass to add color and authenticity to your book. Add dry or otherwise preserved natural plant materials to the pages, complete your journaling, and then add your photographs after you get back home.

Leaves adhered to the page with gel medium are the only embellishments this photo needs. The purchased photo mat and rub-on letters complete this photo taken by Laura Jean Davis.

Tip

If the plant material you collect is larger than your Scrapbook on the Go page, shape it to fit your page before you microwave it.

This kudzu page from my Field Notes book was fast and easy to complete. I coated the background with matte medium, carefully placed the kudzu, and then gently applied matte medium to the surface of the plant material with my fingers.

Fast-and-easy titles and hand-drawn lines, using a plain #2 pencil

Leaves collected from a fall morning walk were dried and arranged on this home-based Scrapbook on the Go. I coated the background with matte gel medium, carefully positioned the leaves, and then gently applied matte gel medium to the surface of the leaves with my fingers. I added some stamped images around the leaves for additional background interest.

When placing heavy or bulky items in your Scrapbook on the Go, use a heavy-duty adhesive like The Ultimate! to hold them securely. Allow glue to dry thoroughly before handling.

I used wire to hold this piece of driftwood in Field Notes. The acorns were sanded down to make them a bit smaller.

Some natural materials are already dry when you collect them. Driftwood, shells, and pebbles all can be successfully added to your project. The board book base of Field Notes helps support the extra weight.

You don't have to travel to enjoy making a Scrapbook on the Go. I made this Backyard Field Guide one beautiful weekend spent at home. Plant materials, feathers, flowers, photos, and vintage plant guides all joined together with rubber stamps and rub-on letters in this sweet accordion book.

Ribbon, buttons, and other simple embellishments complete this spread. The pink paper heart was cut freehand, crumpled, and then lightly touched with a stamp pad to add interest. Leave room—in this case it's the pink heart—for someone to journal personal thoughts about the guest or event.

Photographs by Laura Jean Davis

SHAPIN' up

Technique:
Working With an Unusual Shape

Not all of your Scrapbook on the Go projects need to be square or rectangular. Think about all the great shapes available in tins and boxes that could be converted into a future project. How about converting a metal CD carrying case into a Scrapbook on the Go project for a music-loving teenager? Just create a round page template, and you'll be ready to rock 'n' roll!

 When working in any shaped board book, cut or tear your background paper larger than the book page or spread. After gluing in the paper—I use a glue stick—use the outer edge of the board book as your cutting guide for trimming away the excess paper. This will eliminate the frustration of trying to align your background paper with your book base. Use scissors, a craft knife, or a rotary cutter. Be sure to protect your work surface from sharp cutting tools, and keep the tools safely away from other people.

 When working in a shaped tin, create a template for your "pages." Trace around the container onto a piece of mat board, cardboard, or poster board. Carefully cut out your shape inside the tracing lines so that the completed template will fit inside the container. I like to create a "window" template at the same time to isolate sections of photos and layouts for cropping to the desired shape.

Inspiration: The Bridal Shower

WHAT I USED

Before I Left Home

- A heart-shaped blank board book from C&T Publishing

- Scrapbook paper from The Paper Loft and Scenic Route Paper Co.

 With the guest of honor's permission, trim words or images from some of the gift cards to incorporate into the special Scrapbook on the Go.

For an extra special party book, have the guests sign their names in the book. Create a page for everyone to sign, or have people sign next to a photo of themselves.

At the Event

- A digital camera and photo printer

- Wrapping paper to support the theme

- Ribbon from the packages

- Small stamp pad to enhance edges

- Adhesive—double-stick tape or a glue stick

- Scissors—straight or decorative edges

- Embellishments—brads, label holders, tags, metal charms, buttons, rub-on letters, or words with an appropriate theme

A great photograph, mini–file folders and tags from Li'l Davis, preprinted and gift package ribbons, rub-on words, and some small embellishments create this happy spread. The tags offer personal journaling space.

 Leave room for the guest of honor and other party guests to journal in your Scrapbook on the Go gift book. Tags, mini file folders, small pieces of lined paper, and mini library card pockets all create wonderful places to tuck in handwritten notes.

The front cover of *The College Search*

Long time comin'

Technique: Long-Term Projects

If you're anything like I am, you get caught up in wanting to finish a project before it's ready to be finished. Not all of our scrapbooks need to cover a finite period of time. Instead of trying to finish your book ASAP, what if you looked at some of your Scrapbook on the Go projects as long-term commitments? Sometimes working on a project over a longer period of time and holding all of those moments together in one book is the perfect organizational solution.

Okay, you're thinking, "What is she talking about?" Here are some examples of events or projects that I think would be great candidates for longer-term projects.

- Instead of incorporating Boy Scout or Girl Scout activities into your child's regular scrapbook, how about dedicating a Scrapbook on the Go to this purpose? Include many years' worth of Scout outings and camping trips all in one book.

- How about the years of dance lessons, piano recitals, or sports activities? No, you won't always be creating at the event, but the energy of adding a page or spread when there is a new "installment" will fuel your enthusiasm for the book, and you'll be creating an interesting timeline of similar activities. It's a great way to see growth, maturity, and progress within a limited subject matter.

Planning a longer-term Scrapbook on the Go project entails special considerations. At the beginning of the project, you probably won't know exactly how many pages or spreads you'll want in your book. Choosing a format that is flexible is the key to success here. This chipboard book was perfect. I can add or subtract manila pages to suit my needs as I work in the book.

Inspiration: The College Search

My long-term Scrapbook on the Go project is *The College Search*. It's definitely been more than just a one-day or one-week event, and it's been great fun for me to document our daughter's visits to different campuses.

WHAT I USED
Before I Left Home

- A chipboard book and some embellishments from Li'l Davis

- A JustRite Stamper to stamp the title of the book

- Paper from The Paper Loft cut down to be slightly smaller than the book pages

Tip An important consideration for a long-term project is durability. As you'll be working over a period of time, don't start with a fragile book. Make sure you choose something sturdy that can be handled a lot and that will accommodate your needs as you continue to add to it.

On the Road

- Metal frames, tags, and library card pockets from Li'l Davis

- A digital camera and photo printer

- Papers from The Paper Loft

- A glue stick

- Scissors

- Ribbon, hand-dyed twill from Scenic Route Paper Co., and other fibers

- A Ranger Distress Ink pad in antique linen color

- Rub-on letters from Making Memories

- A pen for journaling

- Photo corners

- Packing tape for transfers

- Paper ephemera collected from college brochures

21 AUGUST 2005

Here's the first spread in the book. On the back of the cover, I collaged college names torn from brochures and glued in place. The other side of the spread has two tags. The "Are You Ready?" phrase from one of the brochures grabbed me right away. I journaled my feelings about my daughter preparing to move away to school and gave her the other tag to complete. For the fibers in the tags, I combined hand-dyed twill and torn fabric strips from a quilt shop I found on one of the tour trips.

In any college brochure, you'll find lots of text, images, emblems, and other details that you can include in your Scrapbook on the Go.

VISITING HARVARD

What other types of books might work for a long-term project? How about using a loose-page "not-a-book-at-all" format for a long-term Scrapbook on the Go project? Or make a tag book, like *Evidence*, shown on page 57. You can adapt it to suit yourself.

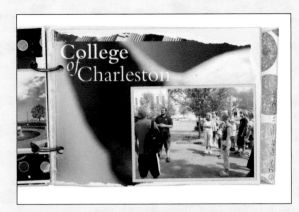

Tearing part of the College of Charleston brochure created the perfect background for the campus tour photo.

Tearing, cutting, and layering all come together in this Grinnell College spread.

It's still a work in progress, but I love how full this book is getting to be! It'll be a bittersweet moment for me when I finish the last page, where I plan to feature whichever school Emma decides to attend.

Using wallet-size photos on this spread allowed me to include more photographs. Check with your photo processor (or check your manual if you own a portable photo printer) to see about size options.

bLaNk slates

Technique: Blank Books

Want to get a head start on your future scrapbook projects? Ever need a gift ready at a moment's notice? Do you like to recycle? Do you have lots of scrapbook papers that you haven't used yet? If you answered yes to at least one of these questions, this section has some fast and easy ideas.

All of the examples in this chapter can be used to create your own ready-to-use Scrapbook on the Go bases. Some are as quick as buying a book and some scrapbook paper, adding a few embellishments, and being ready to head out the door. Others give you an opportunity to recycle supplies you have around your home or office.

All of these ideas are wonderful to use as a starting point for gifts. Maybe your friends admire your scrapbooks but haven't gotten into scrapbooking yet themselves. What better way to jump-start friends than by presenting them with a custom-made Scrapbook on the Go?

What are you waiting for? Let's get to it!

Buying a pre packaged assortment of scrapbook papers will give you a great start on any Scrapbook on the Go project. You can always add more scrapbook papers for additional variety.

When making a Scrapbook on the Go to give as a gift, use colors that you know the recipient likes. If you have no idea what the recipient's color preferences are, use a limited or neutral palette.

Inspiration: The Whole Kit 'n' Caboodle

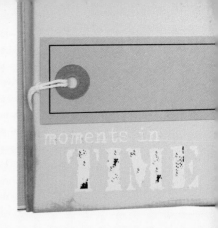

WHAT I USED

- A blank book

- Assorted scrapbook papers

- Stamp pads for adding color to some page edges

- Embellishments—brads, label holders, tags, buttons, pockets, envelopes, mini accordion folded–paper, rub-ons with a general theme, slide pockets, ribbons, and charms

- Adhesive—a glue stick or Xyron

- Scissors—straight or decorative edges

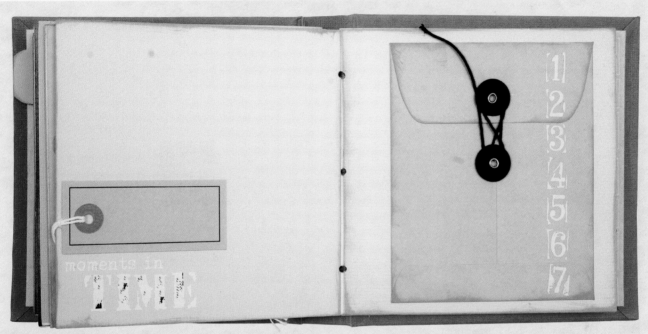

Be sure to include an envelope or pocket somewhere in your blank slate book to collect ephemera, tuck journaling, or keep extra photos safe.

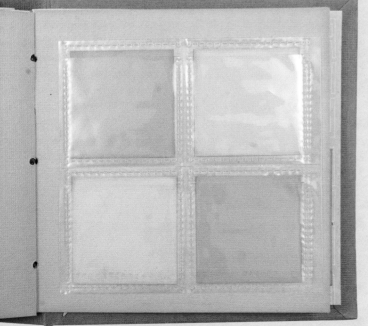

Jump-start any spread by recycling clear plastic slide holders. Add squares of scrapbook paper, and you have a perfect page to feature small collected items, cropped photographs, foreign coins, or other special finds.

Tip

Consider adding a small assortment of extras when you give someone a Scrapbook on the Go blank slate, especially if the person is new to scrapping. A few brads, some ribbons, tiny envelopes, charms, buttons, and so on will inspire the recipient, and you'll have a new scrapping buddy!

Inspiration: Brown Baggin' It

Brown Baggin' It is a fun idea for a Scrapbook on the Go designed for you or to give as a gift. Embellish most or all of the pages, and then simply tuck your photos and ephemera into the many pockets. Or leave more of the pages blank to add your photos as you travel. Either way, this paper bag book is fun and easy to complete ahead of time.

WHAT I USED

I started with a Paper Bag Book kit from Altered Pages (see Sources on page 63). The kit included brown paper lunch bags, several scrapbook papers, vintage images, stickers, a small stamp pad, and lots of embellishment options.

- Embellishments—many of these came with the kit (If you're making up your own or simply want to add more variety, consider brads, clips, stickers, buttons, ribbons, twill tape, rubber stamps to support your theme, pockets, envelopes, page and photo corners, label holders, etc.)
- Adhesive—glue stick or Xyron
- Scissors—straight or decorative edges

Note

Paper lunch bags are not acid free.

I combined several items from the kit for the cover of my paper bag book. A vintage image, some scrapbook paper, and a metal bookplate made this a quick and fun start for my project.

Tip
Not all of the pockets in a paper bag book need to open to the side. You might want to glue, tape, or otherwise close off the end and cut a slit along the top edge of the bag to create a different kind of pocket.

I stamped the car collage and paired it with some vintage-car scrapbook paper for the base of this spread. I created a top-opening pocket and inserted a large tag. Add some ribbon, a small envelope to include coins, and a couple of other embellishments, and you'll be ready to hit the road at a moment's notice.

Scrapbook paper, vintage images, and a blank coaster highlighted with a stamp pad complete this funky spread. You can see the opening of the paper bag just waiting to hold more ephemera.

For this large pocket, I covered a CD sleeve with scrapbook paper and ribbons. It's easy, fast, and strong enough to hold lots of ephemera or photographs, or to conceal journaling that you don't want others to know about.

I created a large slide holder using a rubber stamp and cardboard to give it dimension. Adding a library card pocket and decorative scrapbook tapes creates a spread that is ready to hold your memories.

Tip I chose to fold my paper bag book down the center of the bags and then sewed them together with my sewing machine. You could glue them together, or use eyelets to reinforce punched holes and bind them with fibers.

I added ribbons and buttons to the binding of my paper bag book. It's ready for just about any future Scrapbook on the Go project.

More Ideas for *Brown Baggin' It*

- If you want more space for your ephemera, create larger pockets by binding the bags at their bases instead of down their centers.

- Punch holes in the ends of the bags, reinforce them with eyelets, and string them on loose-leaf binder rings.

- Embellish the loose-leaf rings with ribbon, yarn, string, charms, or key chains.

- Use large binder clips to bind your Scrapbook on the Go— put a date on each bag so you can put it back in chronological order after showing it off to friends and family.

- Have a coil binding attached at the copy shop. It's not expensive.

- Collage the outside of the brown paper bags, and keep the rest of your collected ephemera and photos in them. One bag for each day is easy!

These paper bag projects are so fun and fast to complete that they make a perfect gift. You won't have so many hours tied up in their creation that you are unwilling to part with one. Better yet, make two of them at a time. Keep one, and give one to a traveling companion for a personal Scrapbook on the Go.

Embellished envelopes make an inexpensive, quick, and fun Scrapbook on the Go. They can also keep your ephemera organized.

Envelopes

Have fun with colors, shapes, and sizes. Mix and match them for a unique Scrapbook on the Go, or stick with a single color and shape to suit your mood. Before your trip or event, set aside an hour to prepare this book, and you'll be ready to create a unique, easy Scrapbook on the Go.

WHAT YOU'LL NEED

- Envelopes
- Small pieces of scrapbook paper
- Adhesive—a glue stick is fine
- Eyelets—be sure they are large enough to accommodate the binder rings
- Office supply store binder rings
- Scissors

Envelopes with a straight-flap edge are easiest to use for this technique.

HOW TO MAKE THE BOOK

1. Trace the flap of your envelope onto a piece of scrap paper to make your pattern long enough that your scrapbook paper covers both sides of the flap and wraps around to the back of the envelope about 1″.

In addition to adding a custom decorative element to your envelopes, the layering of paper also prevents the envelope from accidentally sealing itself and adds strength to the flap so it will be able to withstand the extra handling it will receive.

Embellish the ends of some of the envelopes. The straight edge flaps of these envelopes make them easy to cover.

2. Trace your template onto your papers, and cut out the papers.

3. Apply adhesive from a glue stick to the back of the paper, and then apply it to the envelope flap and wrap it around. Repeat for each envelope.

4. Use a punch to make holes near the end of your envelopes and secure the eyelets.

5. Thread the envelopes onto the binder rings.

Option

Add embellishments as desired.

If you are using these envelopes to temporarily keep your ephemera organized, put dates or place names on the flaps. Or number them to correlate with the number of days in your trip.

Inspiration: Evidence

Here's another fast, easy project that combines my love of recycling with an opportunity to use all kinds of cool papers and embellishments. This project is also wonderfully adaptive to your needs. Just add or take away pages as your Scrapbook on the Go develops. This "book" is also another fast and easy gift idea. Let's start playing!

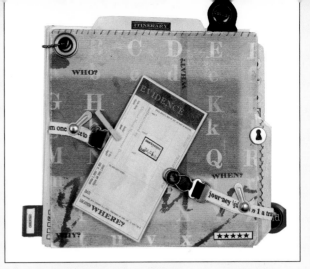

The front cover of *Evidence* is embellished with all kinds of fun doodads.

WHAT YOU'LL NEED

- Recycled manila file folders as the bases for this fun Scrapbook on the Go

- Scrapbook paper and embellishments (The ones shown are all from 7gypsies; I used their color washes, metal embellishments, printed twill tape, garter hooks, tags, rub-on words, stickers, clips, and fabric embellishments.)

- Adhesives—glue stick and The Ultimate! adhesive

- Large eyelets or grommets for "binding" the book

- Binder rings or old-fashioned ball chains to hold the pages together

HOW TO MAKE THE BOOK

1. Cut your file folders to the size you want the pages to be. My pages are about 8″ square. I left some of the file folder tabs on for fun.

2. Cut pieces of scrapbook paper smaller than your file folder pages.

3. Glue the scrapbook paper to the file folder base. Glue some straight and some off-kilter for extra interest.

4. Embellish the pages with things like metal, paper, and fabric while still leaving places to add photos and other embellishments when you complete your Scrapbook on the Go.

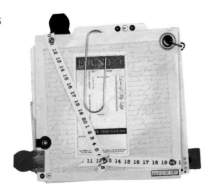

5. On the back cover of *Evidence,* I created a twill-tape holder for a tag, photograph, or other ephemera.

6. Repeat for as many pages as you want in your book.

7. Decide what order you want the pages to be in.

8. Punch holes to accommodate your grommets, and hammer the grommets in place.

9. Thread the pages onto large loose-leaf binder rings or use ball chains, as shown.

When you spread out *Evidence* in front of you, you'll have all the proof you need that this is a fun project you'll want to make.

This irresistible book is ready for any collection of evidence. It is a great project for incorporating found objects and a wide variety of ephemera. Get together with some scrapping friends, and pool your collections to start your next unique Scrapbook on the Go.

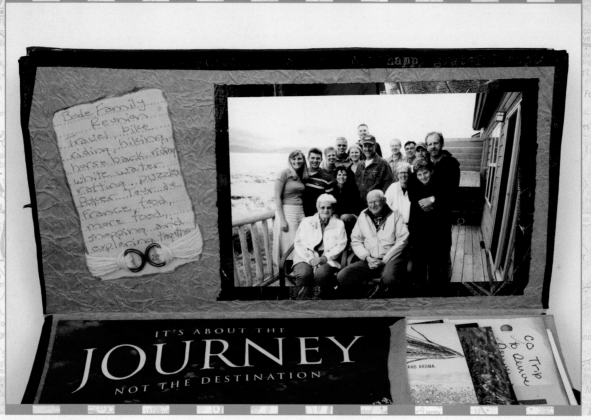

party time!

Technique: Party Time Ideas

Opportunities for celebratory Scrapbooks on the Go are endless: retirement parties, birthdays, family reunions, anniversary celebrations, wedding and baby showers. . . . You'll save money and create a very special gift!

For any party-themed Scrapbook on the Go, decide before the event what you will use for your backgrounds. Are you going to add scrapbook paper for the backgrounds before you get to the party, or would you rather wait until some gifts have been opened and recycle some of the gift wrap for the backgrounds?

Tip For an extra special party theme book, have the guests sign their names somewhere in the book, either next to their photos or on a page you create for everyone to sign.

Are you thinking that you won't have time to Scrapbook on the Go while attending a birthday party, retirement party, family reunion, or wedding or baby shower? Think again! Arm yourself with a digital camera and portable photo printer, and make the most of party time. Create the backgrounds and embellish them with decorations such as ribbons while the guest is opening presents or while everyone is socializing. Recruit another guest to take digital photos of the festivities (be sure the guest knows how to use your camera).

When everyone breaks for refreshments, review the photos, choose your favorites, and then let the printer do the work while you join the refreshment line. Simply add the printed photos to the book and present it to the guest of honor as your very special gift. I can guarantee your gift won't be duplicated!

ABOVE: Be sure to take group photos whenever practical. Use the self-timer on someone's camera if no one is available to shoot a group photo for you. Instead of each guest using a separate camera and taking multiple shots—wearing out everyone's smile in the process—ask a responsible photographer in the group to take the photos and make copies of the best shot or email it to everyone so each guest receives a copy.

Inspiration: Birthday Box

WHAT I USED
Before I Left Home

- A recycled box and part of a set of recycled flashcards (I lightly sanded the box and several of the cards to make them more receptive to adhesives.)

 Tip For little ones who don't write, bring a child-safe stamp pad, and have them add their thumbprints to one of the party pages. Use a damp cloth to wipe any excess ink off their fingers before they run off to play some more.

At the Party

- A digital camera and portable printer

- Recycled gift wrap, tissue papers, and gift cards (You could buy some ahead of time if you'd rather.)

- Hand-dyed twill tape from Scenic Route Paper Co.

- Rub-on letters and words from Making Memories

- Ranger Distress Ink pad in Weathered Wood color

- Embellishments—metal label holder, various ribbons, mini-brads, eyelets, and metal photo turners

- A Fastenater stapler and decorative staples from EK Success

- A glue stick

- Scissors

 **Tip** Leave room for the guest of honor and other party guests to journal in your Scrapbook on the Go gift book. Tags, mini file folders, small pieces of lined paper, and mini library card pockets all create wonderful places to tuck handwritten notes.

Following the Texture Time technique (page 28), I adhered the tissue papers to the cards. Gluing the excess tissue to the backs of the cards was fast and easy. Because the tissue is so thin and flexible, it was happy to follow the rounded contour of the corners. I arranged these adorable photos and embellishments to make this birthday set. I simply covered the box with glue stick adhesive and then layered it with tissue paper before I added the lightly sanded gift card and ribbons.

Birthday party photos by Laura Jean Davis

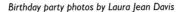

 WiSH you were here

Technique:
Working the Postal Service

Really don't want to spend your time away from home making your Scrapbook on the Go? Trying to pack light and can't imagine packing anything extra? Here's a great project that requires very little of you while you're away, yet gives you an excellent opportunity to remember the details of your trip. You don't even need a camera for this Scrapbook on the Go! All you'll need is some spare change and a pen. Buy yourself postcards of the sights, and you'll have a custom Scrapbook on the Go started before you get home!

While you're waiting for lunch, or the train, or when you're back in your room in the evening, write the postcards. Address them to yourself and drop them in the mail the next time you pass a mailbox and you've completed a page in your Scrapbook on the Go! Once you're back home, collect all the postcards and relive your trip as you put them in chronological order. Yes, it's that simple!

 Be sure that any family members left at home know to keep the postcards that arrive before you do.

 If you're going to be in the same country for several days, estimate how many postcards you'll be sending, and purchase all the stamps you'll need at once. This way you won't have to hunt for stamps during your excursions, and if you don't speak the local language, you won't have to deal with an awkward situation again. If you are unable to overcome the language barrier, simply carry in a postcard, point to the stamp position and the destination country, and hold up your fingers to indicate how many you'd like to buy.

I recycled manila file folders to make the "binding" for my Wish You Were Here Italy postcard project. I cut strips that were 5½" x the width of the file folder, used a bone folder (or the back of a large spoon) to make crisp, accordion folds, and with acrylic paints and brayers, I painted the sturdy manila stock to remind me of the colors of Italy.

Both sides of each postcard are visible, so you'll be able to read your journaling entries from every stop along the way.

Buttons, beads, photo corners, hand stitches, and eyelets are all simple fasteners for attaching the postcards to the accordion-fold "binding."

finishing touches

I hope you'll really enjoy the process of creating your Scrapbook on the Go. I have found so much satisfaction in being able to share my experience or trip with someone very shortly after I get home, while my enthusiasm from the trip is still high—and while I can still engage others in the conversation without the dreaded "let me show you my pictures" attitude. The Scrapbook on the Go is a friendly format. It doesn't intimidate people the way a huge 12" × 12" scrapbook does, and it's much more portable for taking in your bag next time you meet up with some friends.

Remember that early on we discussed your Scrapbook on the Go kit? I mentioned then that you don't have to have everything with you when you are away from home. As soon as you are able once you return home, set aside a few minutes—try not to take more than an hour—to add a few finishing touches to your book. Add those last photos that you just got developed, enhance some pages with some additional embellishments that you didn't have with you, and print out any computer journaling that you want to include. Journal some thoughts about the entire experience, and tuck them into a pocket or envelope. Then go through your leftover collection of ephemera from the trip. One last time, look through it and see if you want to include anything else in your Scrapbook on the Go. Add what you want to, and then, most important, throw away the leftovers. If they weren't good enough to include in your project or even to tuck into a pocket or envelope in your book, they certainly don't need to be taking up space on a closet shelf. Trust me: it'll feel great to get rid of it all now that your Scrapbook on the Go is officially finished!

One final important step:

Sign your work!

And now your Scrapbook on the Go is ready to share!